Bird Flying through the Banquet

Judy Kronenfeld

FUTURECYCLE PRESS
www.futurecycle.org

Library of Congress Control Number: 2016963549

Copyright © 2017 Judy Kronenfeld
All Rights Reserved

Published by FutureCycle Press
Lexington, Kentucky, USA

ISBN 978-1-942371-23-6

For Anya, Zaid, Nadia, and Owen

Contents

Lives of the Dead

My Long-Left Birth City

gleams in a movie,
its lights gems on the plush display
cloth of night, its bridges bracelets.
Yet the shabbiness of a glimpsed
street corner is what gets through,
and mine reaches out from memory to me—
a speaker of its native language—
with *this* begrimed cornice,
this lintel, *this* rain- and sun-mottled awning
over the drugstore window,
this black ash on the sill.
                              As if,
were I to rush there, I could hold
in my hands their distilled atmosphere—
the way someone holds, in the cup
of her ear, a taped voice
achingly familiar. As if
every place we've ever called home
does not flow away from us
on an unlooped conveyer—
like the waters of an infinity pool
vanishing over the zero edge.
As if I wanted to reach down
on my chest for the key there
six decades past, to unlock the square skates,
tighten them against my sneakers, lean in
and rumble over the cracked sidewalks flashing mica
from the drugstore to the park,
and glide on its paths and stop
at another corner,
newsstand, candy store, barber shop—
utterly, beautifully, unremarkable.

Immigrant Silences

—on finding my long-dead mother's transit passport

Here she is:
plump in a high-sheen floral
blouse in the stamped picture,
traveling through *Schweiz*
from *Wien* to *Cherbourg,*
towards that never-discussed passage
to New York. *Haare: schwartz,*
wild as horses' and as coarse,
Augen: dunkel under the cloud
of her adolescent brow,
and glittery with angst I recognize.

It's as if she's back from a past
that had been masked by witness protection,
from the *then*
for which I have no other photo
and so few of her words (I barely
asked)—
from what she was
before naturalized my Mother,
American Stella...

Stella, why did you never tell me
Sara was your given name? Or why
my grandparents—gone
before I was born—obtained
Quota Immigration Visa No. 464,
August 1, 1927? Broken windows?
Cartoons with side-curls
and long noses? Did your family blanch
or scoff?

Sara, did you sigh, relieved,
or did you weep from fear
and grief as the train wound past
the peasant-postcard
meadows, past Wagnerian gaps
with alpen rose and edelweiss-
splashed high crags, and you left Vienna
behind forever: the solemn
facades and statues,
the modest snug rooms across the canal
from the Stephanskirche (so cold
and grand), the neighbors
who smiled the Jewish child in
for Christmas cake?

I will never know. Though I once saw
the tiny circle of park
near *Zwei Ilgplatz* (the address you never
forgot)—its soil blackened
with dog turds, splattered
with greenly iridescent dog piss,
so close to the frankincense and myrrh
of the confectioner's window,
the marzipan rabbits
and the shining Easter eggs.

Neighborly Sorrow

July 7, 2005, and for the first time—
perhaps because my father this year
stepped into eternity to join her—
I light a yahrzeit candle for my mother,
ten years dead, the homely
Manischewitz glass filled
with a day's worth of white wax
surprising me at my local supermarket.
The label's Hebrew letters,
segmented like insect legs,
look mysterious and familiar
as my vanished girlhood, when,
according to some secret
algorithm, she'd purchase these
jars—so cheaply utilitarian,
so readily available—or take one
from a cupboard, cover her head
with faded kerchief
and pray, swaying, weeping names
I didn't know.

Those candles (she never bought
just one) made me feel that sorrow
was a dime a dozen in a Jewish
house, that it always hung around,
like a neighbor with nothing better
to do, one who protests she's on a diet,
but mooches cake and coffee,
and gossips in the kitchen
all afternoon...

How strange that such a flame
burns now in my agnostic
house, three thousand miles

from the Bronx, and that I've mumbled
some transliterated words over it,
after googling *Yizkor.*
"May her soul be bound...
together with the souls of...
Sarah, Rebecca, Rachel and Leah..."
Sarahle, Rivka, Rachele...!
So that was her prayer!
The past creeps, light
as summer duskfall, over
the hairs of my neck.

My husband laughs at me
for going New Age with
candle flame. I don't admit
how comforting it was to have,
glowing on our mantel, the tall blue glass
candle the Temple gave us (when we appeared
for my mother's funeral)—to catch a glimpse
of shadows bobbling on the wall,
to think of the flame
from another room, to know
it was there, breathing—
as if her soul that whole week flickered
at some way station...

I keep checking this flame now
as if looking in on a visitor I hope
will linger. After almost two days,
it floats on a mere quarter-inch
of melted paraffin in the ordinary
glass—neither brazen,
nor golden—like those she used to wash
and save.

Values

My mother's couch was nouveau middle-class
"Italian provincial antique white and deluxe gold
brocade," immobilized in thick, glossy
plastic that stuck to your thighs in summer
and made you sweat; you peeled yourself
off it, dripping, and it screaked.

Achieved after decades of forlorn
secondhand, in her late
middle age, after I left home—
the couch of someone who had waited
dusty years for it, and knew that time
would never grant such a one again,
the gift that never stopped giving,
new each morning, the plastic glinting—
it remained on display in my parents'
one-bedroom New York apartment
like a never-eaten white-gold passion-
fruit genoise under a clear cake
dome.

And if it was a shrine, a symbol, the butt
of exasperated jokes, and only in winter,
a bearable place to sit (when your legs
were protected by thick pants
or skirts), and, even then, your purchase
was sketchy, you felt you might
slide off, so what?

When we flew East for the visit
my mother had long sought,
her small grandson, exhausted
by the trip and the heat,
was put down for the night

on that couch—which she'd covered
with crisp sheets. She closed the Venetian
blinds, and we were all shushed.
He squirmed as we spoke in whispers—
my husband and I on the humble
guest hide-a-bed, my folks
on two dining chairs turned toward us—
then, thumb in mouth, nestled in,
rump up, legs tucked under, sheets bunching
under his round pot. A half-hour
later, he was on the floor, bawling,
though unhurt, having slid
off that couch on the water-slide
slick it secreted.

My mother rushed over, brushed back
the curls that plastered his glistening
forehead, kissed his bright red cheek
and said: "I'm stripping the couch cover off."

We tried and tried to dissuade her,
suggested a pallet on the floor. But
no go. Bleary-eyed, our son sat on the rug,
while we helped with the divestment—
feeling oddly depleted, as when something
you thought you dearly wanted fails
to bring joy. New sheets were spread,
our boy put down in thick briefs.

An hour later, when, again, he woke,
the not unexpected yellow blush,
the baptized white brocade.

"Bubbele!" my mother cried,
and pressed her sopping grandson to her,
as if he'd accomplished something
great.

Unimaginable

*Though I recall that moment [of his baby's death] with
absolute crushing clarity, it is still unimaginable to me.*
—Aleksandar Hemon, "A Tale of Two Daughters"

Just out of "successful"
surgery on the hip she broke
after her second stroke, my mother
asked for a comb and a mirror
and said, for the thousandth time,
"I look like a prune"—

unlike the faceless,
the deformed, the knowingly terminally
ill, the body-debasing, who have learned,
or been forced, to think of themselves
as souls. Death was not yet
close as her coat, wasn't
sleeping with her, lived
in another country, reachable only
by an arduous, and as yet unplanned
journey.

And that's when we can
imagine it—isn't it?—whether it's ours,
or even—God help us—a child's. Mahler said
he couldn't have written
the *Kindertotenlieder* after his child
had died, though he'd *imagined* his child
had died, in order to write. But before,
just a touch Romantic, isn't it,
à la Père Lachaise—the caped
and draped figures, streaked with corroded
tears, the small child, head rolled back
in final grimace, held aloft
in the angel's arms—

My mother might have imagined
triumphant vindication *à la*
Ann Landers—*Guilty and Heartbroken*
Daughter writes *Now my mother is gone*
and I'm racked with remorse.

But I wasn't.
I did what I could.
I brought the comb and mirror.
I put them away. I sat by the bed.
I held the fingers that dripped over
its side, and she whispered
"my angel" as she slid.

My lucky mother
put down the mirror, clucking.
No slow striptease of the mortal, no
death mask, no practice coffin, no hot
death breath prickling the back
of her neck. She said to oblivion
"Not me!" and to us: "God doesn't
want me yet." And the next
day: mugger death in the dark alley—
one quick rap to the back of the head.

Stirring Banana-Bread Batter
with My Mother's Spoon

Dumb, humble wooden spoon—
a little old-fashioned knob
on the handle—probably nearing
a hundred years old, dumb
through thousands and thousands
of turns of the wrist as she mixed chopped eggs,
blintz filling, noodle pudding, gefilte fish,
too dumbly useful to ever
have been replaced or updated,
mine now for almost a generation:
what does it say, the spoon I saved
because it was hers, the spoon
that will survive, though cracked,
gouged, stained, bleached?

It is rinsed now,
cool on the inside
and so smooth.
I move its bowl, still smelling
of the essence of banana,
across my lips. As if it could
caress, as if it could speak
into my mouth,
as if it could change
its imperturbable long-lastingness
quiet as hers.

Routine Blood Work

The nurse said, smiling, "This will just take a minute, Mr. Z. Please put your arm on this armrest," and I lifted my father's forearm gently onto the board. She said, "You look like a very nice gentleman, Mr. Z," and glanced, kindly, at me, after tying the tourniquet around his withered biceps, palpating and swabbing the inside of his arm, and guiding the needle into a vein. Two years before this moment, he would have smiled a little brave self-mocking smile, just for me, or to ingratiate himself with the nurse; a year before, he would have said "OUCH!," like a small boy who'd been misled; a few months before, his "OUCH!" would have momentarily awakened him from sleep. "Thank you, Mr. Z. You're a very good patient," the nurse said, carefully releasing the tourniquet so it wouldn't smack his skin, then smoothing out a Band-Aid in the crook of his elbow, and I kissed the top of my father's head that slumped on his chest, and returned his flaccid arm to his lap.

Nothing to Worry About

"Nothing to worry about,"
dad used to say on the phone,
even while he told me mom
was in the hospital again—
his desire to appease
my racing heart racing ahead
of realities.
"Nothing to
worry about," he'd repeat,
hearing my sharp
intake of breath.

Before long I'd have to fly
home: two sick kids
on my hands. She'd become
desperately ill; he'd
broken down.

But his first impulse
was to be a gate, like the one
at the little tots' playground,
that will not let
big troubles in.

And now all gates
are gone. Fear
rolls into town like a military convoy,
and no one's at the crossing,
wavering out into the middle
of the road, to hold up
his flimsy
Stop.

Lives of the Dead

Alive in my dream, and serene,
they sit in our old 40-watt-
dim Bronx kitchen on the lollipop-red
dinette set leatherette chairs. On the table,
of all things, a game of Scrabble,
though neither dad nor mom could spell.
I've just come up from "downstairs,"
where someone brandishing an AK-47
stepped out of an armored pick-up
and grabbed the grocery money
in my fist, but let me run off,
someone out of a conflict somewhere—
Ukraine, Pakistan, Iraq, Syria, Gaza?
Living room newly redone in deep
forest green and wine (hide-a-bed
gone), the only bedroom (no longer mine)
now in chenille, but all the rooms
still in the '50s, and I'm visiting
from the 2010s. My father wants to know
if I'd like to play, though I'm frantic.
I yell, "I must contact the authorities!"
Studying his tiles, he says to call
the operator, and points at the black
rotary phone without breaking
his gaze. With a satisfied nod
he puts down a triple-word score,
nudels, and my mother, poker-faced,
trumps him with seven-lettered *brockly*—
both of them comfortable and anarchic
in their little pocket of moored time.

Ten Minutes

My father always set the alarm
ten minutes early—4:50 instead of
5:00 a.m.—so he could fall back
into a hazy sleep on the hide-a-bed
in the living room. Perhaps he was gentling
himself, showing himself a deliberate
kindness, by adding a step
between oblivion and the icy jolt
of another exhausting day. Perhaps his sleep
was made that much more delicious
because he was almost conscious of it,
almost enjoyed the sensation of sleeping
while sleeping, thought *ah, ten...nine...eight...seven
more long minutes* (as I did, following his lead
on interminable high school mornings), before,
rank with sleep sweat, he sat
a few seconds in striped boxers
and ribbed undershirt, then hauled
himself up to shower in our tiny
bathroom, humid with laundry,
and get dressed for work.

It's terrifying how far back
this memory goes. I feel as if
I've had to lie on my belly
with a head lamp and inch forward
in the dark to *see* it. And now I grab hold
of it, as if he could have ten minutes
again, and I could grant them because
I remember how he treasured them:
ten minutes good as pre-dinner cupcakes for a kid
who's been bullied at school when at last

he's home; ten more minutes
of breathing, for me to see him,
nine, eight, seven, six—as if
ten minutes would sweeten arm-twisting
death, or gentle me into braving his.

Generations

Clambering up my front steps, grocery sacks
throttling my icy fingers, weirdly
agitated. Habit throwback?
Hated anticipating the blinking machine
before the parents passed on—
so many messages "just checking in." But maybe
it's excitement. When I open
the door: only the landline's intense
quiet, into which I feel sucked
as if I could disappear.

Until you call, child, on my cell,
after so many weeks,
and like a creature returned
home, after languishing far away
from its ecological niche, I fall into the rooms
of your voice, sprawling on the den floor
of your familiar timbre. You laugh
your delicious laugh, dishing
on a childless friend who doesn't understand
"the lure of kids." And I'm thinking
Evolution will soon watch me
keel over in the empty nest, and God
write off the entire planet,
not being that into Us. I'm fantasizing relocation
to new solar systems in infinite space-time
where immortality's perfected, quaffing
neuro enhancers to keep my progeny in mind—

"Hold on, Mom."

And—why not?—retroactive resurrection.

The mute landline still seems wired
for the channel of the dead,
who are indwelling, but unhearable,
like the music of one's native tongue.

"Turned up the thermostat, but the kids are still
too cold to nap! C'n I call you back?"

"Of course," I say.

"Talk to you soon."

"Love you. Kiss those babies."

"Will do."

…Daughter, I can almost touch your grandparents' store
of love—a reassurance behind me,
like a stockpile of seasoned wood in readiness
for winters to come.

Yet I imagine the landline rings,
and it's them, on coffee break
from death, and we speak to each other
using your words and mine

Talk to you soon
Love you. Kiss those babies
Will do

syllables haunting
in their minor key—
as aural registers briefly
cross that uncrossable threshold.

Beyond Request

Bread

Even the packaged kind—
twisty tie untwisted—
sends up its yeasty plume
to the nose, its celebration
of morning hunger...

and I think of truckers in a diner,
knuckles greasy, gathering up
the creamy yolks with a crust,
before each climbs alone into his cab,

of a student breaking a bagel
in half as she runs to an early
class to present her report, bits of garlic
pungent on her tongue—

all of us eager as a spaniel
under a table for that leftover rewarding
morsel of toast soaked in the perfume
of sausage or bacon—

how we take the new day
into ourselves, and it crosses
the barriers of our cells
and enters our blood,
how it may feed us,
or not.

Intimacies

Ahead of me, on line in the jammed
food court, where salt and oil rub shoulders
on the air, a boy almost too big
for a man's arms—maybe three
or four—caresses the man's cheeks
with both slow, soft hands, whispering
worshipping words, as if he were kneeling
before an icon in church. The holiness
is almost embarrassing; there's something
pleading and beyond his age, something designed
in the boy's repetitive petting, as if he were
pressing the man into place. And the man
accepts the adoration as coolly as a saint.

How early we learn touch is love: when I held
my two-year-old granddaughter in my arms
to say good-bye for a long time and whispered
"I love you," she stroked my breast twice,
her eyes filling with prescient light.

But this boy—is he trying to bribe
his dad, or step-dad, out of sheer
need, *willing* him to love him,
or to stay, the way kids bend their parents
at the elbows, hips and knees in the dollhouses
of their minds, so no matter how much
the two hate each other, they sit arm-in-arm?

Almost my turn at the counter now;
the man has set the child
down, and he monkey-wraps
around a stalwart jean-clad calf.

I force my eyes away.

Beyond Request

One of the bed pillows—
thin down—
propped upright behind her head
leans over, soft as
snow on snow, and kisses
her waist as she bends forward to lift
her novel from the dresser,

and she thinks
in the second
her eyes close
he's removed a hand
from his mystery
to rest on my lower spine.

It feels anointed
by the free gift
of that grace.

Yet the fingers of both
his hands still grip
the pages
as she straightens up carefully
with her book
against—*oh*—
the doubled pillow.

How naked
her stiffened back
now, in her flannel gown.

All You Need to Know

A new study says cute babies get nicer treatment...
even from Mom.
—*NWI Times*

His sharply angled ferret face
all concentration, a boy in my class
is talking about an image
in someone's poem. He knows
what "faded photographs"
are. His mom was a fox
at twenty, but, now, well,
she's really faded. He'll probably
be ugly when *he's* old, too.
"You're telling us a lot
about yourself," my star student,
cautious, mutters (and for the first time
I notice how regular *his* features). But
the ugly boy's impelled, he *knows*
the truth. "Heck," he almost crows, "I'm ugly
now"— a shrug, a grin,
hazel eyes crinkling smaller,
their yellow lights flashed on...

The beautiful are bored,
the homely bend their gazes
toward their books. I think of mothers
across the globe, in nurseries,
cooing at their pretty
babies, of me in my living room
stroking the dog, whose furry
features pass the test.
"On to the next poem, now?"
I ask, steering past the earnestness
of my ugly student,
and his chameleon, accusing, ugly-beautiful face.

What I Love about New York

August morning, 8:00 a.m., as I clump
off the curb on a Soho street
in my walking sandals, backpack flapping—
the day cloistered with heat,
the glinting sidewalks already
repositories—a woman in a sea-spume
froth of tropical turquoise cocktail dress,
steps off from the south side
towards the north. A slick of sweat
gleams in her puckery crepe-paper
cleavage; under their freight of fantail
lashes, her eyelids beat a syncopated
pulse; her wine-stem ankles alternately
bow slightly out and in as she stutters
across in her four-inch rhinestone-embossed
platform sandals. I can almost hear
the *thwip* as a heel is plucked
out of the ancient dirt between the cobbles—
and I nearly give a "you go girl" nod because
its owner's quest has been so severely
tested. But not utterly crushed.

Hair

1956: the charged air of the "beauty parlor,"
slivered with the acetone of nail polish remover,
flammable with mists of hair spray and silver
and gold highlighters, heavy with the slick
sweetness of pomade, cacophonous with blasts
of hood hair dryers, and fang-nailed women,
fingers held aloft, raising the gossip
decibels as they turn the pages of *True Confessions*
with their wrists. Presiding: the pompadoured hetero
hairdresser—lordly as Monsieur Champagne,
creating towering tresses plied with taffeta
and lace in seventeenth-century Paris—
dallying even with me, barely-into-adolescence,
bestowing hello and good-bye kisses
which promise and seal
the allure for sale.

Fifty years later, at the salon specializing
in the deceptive color that maintains
an illusion of fertile power: still the unasked-for embrace
from the hairdresser, intimate stranger,
co-conspirator, in on the staging,
the props. His manner: a dark comic's,
a doctor's, a date's: first jocular with shaver
in hand ("bare scalp is the new
'crop'"); then patiently listening—a little bit
aloof—to what went awry last time,
what is desired now; then flirtatious,
as if pitching the witchery he's sure
to create.

Monsieur Champagne once turned
on a woman whose hair he'd been assembling,

and told her—wielding stilettos of *tu,*
instead of *vous*—no style would ever
compensate for her huge nose;
then abandoned her—half-concocted—
and walked out.

But my kind coiffeur only inserts
his toweled thumbs a little roughly
into my wet ears, after my shampoo—
as if to dry those whorls gently
was indecorous—and bends
over my lined face to wrap
the towel around my head,
and says nothing to suggest
how much more I need him
than he me.

At the YW Indoor Spa

Like a dog with a warm
tongue, the water licks
their toes. Chrysoprase green,
semi-opaque, it laves
their swollen feet. It bobbles
zipper scars on knees
as they descend—
sideways sometimes, clinging
to the rail, leaving behind
walkers and canes. Rising higher,
it willingly embraces their billowy waists,
their spines, and they sigh,
and briefly close their eyes.

Lily leans into the walking
breaststroke with which they
begin—nippleless in her
maillot, cropped hair
glistening.

From Janet's upper arms raised high
depends an eagle cape of thick
loose flesh—soft
as feathers, mottled, dimpled,
swaying.

Carol's loose suit greyed with use
reveals a swath of pendulous white
belly or pale groin
as she swings her leg open,
closed, open, closed, knee
bent, in the "creaky gate."

On the deck, one of their granddaughters
idles, sliding down in her chair,
the air practicing caresses
as she stretches out her gold
limbs, the hollow of her throat
filling with invisible nectar.

The women in the spa
in their little purdah of no
care—salty as their own
blood—cruise, they ski
(cross-country), they rock
like the nursery horses of their
childhoods, they laugh
about who's been bumped
on *Dancing with the Stars*.

Not Overly Suspicious

Born with a Stainless Steel Spoon in My Mouth

—on scholarship, Smith College, 1962

A distaff Nathan Zuckerman, and no
George Plimpton:

back sore with the weight
of knowledge, as I bike
from the library in the greening almost summer
to my monastic room, gray
with smoke at 2 a.m.,

phosphorescent polka dots
on my palms, pre-exam
notebook pages galvanic
in highlighter neon yellow,
self-correct red and original blue—
popping like Mondrian's *Broadway
Boogie Woogie* in Modern Art
143,

essays punched out
on stiff keys; the holes of the *o*'s
on the Corrasable Bond
almost burnt: a residue
of eraser crumbs
and paper dust,
a two-pack stench
of Merit butts,

and my eyes twitching as if the anxious
engine of my vigorous ambition
had force-marched me past
the dazzling light of closed-door pools
that pierced protective slatted fences,
and strobed my glasses.

The Heresy of Paraphrase

A true poem is...an experience rather than any mere statement
about experience.
—Cleanth Brooks, *The Well Wrought Urn*

"Spit on my face you Jewes, and pierce my side,"
I intone, an acolyte in the garden
of study—Jewish girl from the Bronx
on scholarship at an Ivy college—
kneeling before the vaunted poem.
I am imagining John Donne
imagining the crucifixion, meditating
in my carrel retreat above
the snow-hushed dorms—as Louis Martz said
Donne meditated with the help
of the *Spiritual Exercises of Saint*
Ignatius Loyola in *The Poetry of Meditation*
(Yale U.P., 1954). Toes freezing
in my boots, I give myself
to the text, artifact holy
as a reliquary, *autotelic*—
that word chanted in reverent tones
by Professor R. who's in love with the swirl
of the Baroque, and swirls with it,
his own turns and bows as beautiful,
he knows, as what he bows to.
I am experiencing every phoneme
like blessed wounds; as Donne
becomes Christ—for *"sinnes,*
which passe the Jewes impiety"—
I become him, my voice lowering
to his plangent prayer in the sestet—
"Oh let mee then...admire"—
and not once do I think *Jewes,*
Jews.

Noblesse Oblige

I was well-married as Miranda
to Ferdinand, zippy as Rosalind
in Arden, pony-tailed like a kid,
at my first MLA in 1971, when the handsome
professor of Middle English Lit,
who'd taken to saying in class,
"Feel free to call me Rick!" (was he
newly entering the late '60s zeitgeist?) invited me
to his room on some job-search
pretext. Assuming concern
tantamount to my own
ambitions, I went, not overly
suspicious, and watched while he,
obvious as an undergraduate
cribber, poured more Scotch
than I might drink in a month
of grad-student dinners. But his lips when he
kissed me descended softly
as dewe in Aprille
that falleth on the flowr—their pressure
subtle as the most deft irony.
I helplessly savored
their touch, then begged off,
murmuring something earnest
about loyalty. He asked "Are you
sure?" then let me go,
then said—as my heart fell through all
the stories of myself like an elevator
out of control—"I'll *still* write you
a good letter for that job."

What We're Reduced To

—after the 2012 national political conventions

An early September Monday: we drove on impulse
to a beach in Orange County, away from the viscous,
sulfurous air of our inland valley, smelling of rotten fish—
it turned out—churned up by a storm system
sweeping over the Salton Sea. We tossed into our '97
minivan (dents, chipped paint, tattered Obama stickers)
a beach umbrella inherited from my parents
(its two poles still bearing the Scotch tape
of my father's useless fix) and a couple of new
easy-fold canvas chairs. When we arrived,
thin cloud wisps seemed to stretch
their arms out, respiring; the blue air
was a gift again.

On one of many streets filled with well-kept
houses, neck-on-neck, that didn't shout
their hefty worth, a lucky parking spot,
steps from the steep path to the sand
blessed our impetuous decision. The shine
of breeze-swept light recalled the *luxe* gloss
of the blond college students it had seemed
to blend with, decades before,
when I'd taught, temporarily,
at an O.C. school—a privileged opposite-
of-slumming.

But there were people of color in the surf,
some older folks like ourselves in street clothes,
slipping off outer shirts and shoes, as well
as young girls in bikinis—fat and thin.

We read with the concentration of time out
from time for a few hours in the rigged
umbrella's shade, were soothed by the rhythmic chords

and melodic backwash of the sea, freed a little,
until the sun grew fierce and we plodded
up the slope, then—uh-oh—plucked a note
that had been stuck under our windshield wiper:
GO TAKE YOUR OBAMA AND DIE.

I felt a chill, as if I were a suddenly
feverish child with sunburn she didn't know
she had, after a morning of careless play.
I looked up at the nearest house and this time
saw *his and her walk-in closets, wine cellar, subterranean
seven-car garage.*

And—Ph.D. or not—I *was* my immigrant
parents, shlepping a vinyl hamper of salami
on rye and hard-boiled eggs on a day trip
to Bronx-on-the-Sea, Far Rockaway—
only this was more like they'd taken
a wrong turn to the Hamptons; I belonged again
to people for whom a "beach house"
meant two rented rooms in a ramshackle Victorian
the summers they could afford them,
and grey-faced Daddy taking the train out
Fridays after work for a weekend of *luft.*

My husband, furious, undoubtedly thinking
bitter white guy, rich, or even poor,
scrambled for a pen, and scrawled
under the block letters, nearly breaking its tip:
YOU FIRST, RACIST IDIOT.

Now what? Run to a FedEx
and pamphlet the neighborhood?
We stood with the helpless paper
in his hands. He folded it up
and pushed it into a crevice
on the sidewalk. And we sped
away.

That's an Unusual Name

—Never heard that one before. How did you say
you spell that? C-o-r-n-f-i-e-l-d?
—Not *Cornfield.*
—Whoa! *That's* long.

Praise to the republic of names
with *-chik* or *-chek* or *-nik*
with *shtuh* or *tsuh*
or *-etto* or *-ini,* or *-ez* or *-ero*
or *-feld* or *-berg*

names that sputter
or spritz
with *-owski* or *-ewski*
or *-enski,* or *-zhinsky*
or *-witz*

names that belong
to the great
polysyllabic company
that begins
in one time zone
and ends in another
with *-opolous* or *-amian*
or *-ashvili*
-ayam or *-ootham*
-swami or *-arasamy*

yodel names
like Yudelstein,

names that might choke
the maws of pols and pundits
like chunks of dough—

"Morning, President
Puttermeister," "Nice to see you,
Secretary Svidzinskaia," "Family well,
Senator Sarangarajan?"—

too big to swallow, juicy
names that make you chew
with open mouth,

names that clatter
over the ground
like a toddler's corn-popper
push toy, or quack-and-flap
duck,

thorny-husked durian
names, full of flavor
and funk,

the whole raucous
Babel chorus of them.

The Play of Attention

Brief Reunion

Chugging up and flying down
the hills of San Francisco
in the cab we all squeezed into,
your long woolen thigh
pressed against the thin silk
of mine, your braced arm
blooming above my shoulders like
an arbored vine, I am hushed
as snow, radiant as a body soaking up
the sun, the year cupped
in this quarter-hour, desire
singing singing
its solo aria of praise.

At 70

The gaze and shade of the play
of attention, the gift of Eros (must I
give it up?): absorption of the eyes—

as if a man's could draw
the glistening from my own
like sun

or our glances, intertwined,
were eyebeams traveling
to and fro

transferring "eye-babies,"
as in a poem
by Donne.

What pleasure when such
remembered moments ripple
over my skin

though the *me*
in them has multiply
transmuted

and these new cells
so ineluctably programmed
for demise.

But how disarming
to revive
that picnic table

in the grove—
birches shaking
their shimmering hair,

droplets of light
flying, sun swords,
shade sprinklings,

light like slantwise
golden arrows
in feathered eyes.

Loved Bodies

My dog surrenders
to my hand—
all quiet attention—
his lips blubbering
against its chuff
as I smooth
his snout, his eyes
trembling beneath the palm,
as I stroke his brow

and you, too,
say nothing—
anchoring, for my liberty—
as I finger the mole
above your clavicle,
the deep cleft
in your upper lip,
the little tufts of wild
hair in your ears.

Free-Floating Anxiety

3:00 a.m. again, the hinge
of the universe scrapes,
the house lurches. I was
a jewel in a dark
velvet-lined case, prized,
my light pleasantly muffled,
I was swaddled in plush, my cheek
smooth, but the house
has slipped off its pylons—
I must find the pliers,
the wrenches—the house
has wrenched itself
from foursquare and drifted
to high seas, creaky as a ship
in rough weather, and I—
promoted to captain,
unasked—must tend
to the bridge, the engine,
the load, while the bow,
furious, rises and dips—

Until you awake too,
tired, but measured and calm,
and sigh on your robe,
and lead me below deck,
and turn on the TV. And at last I doze
to the only thing on—
Dunkirk documentaries
in quaint black and white—
my head re-moored
on your shoulder till dawn.

Hokusai's *Under the Wave off Kanagawa*

Like the dugout canoe I watched
the fishermen launch on a beach
in Ghana, decades ago. Straight up
the furious moonlit breakers
they rode, madly paddling,
jerked almost vertical, bouncing
out of their seats, then disappeared
in the hollow of the next wave
and bolted up again.
My young anthropologist husband and I
had both been invited
to ride on the second boat that night
and I had said "yes," fearing my loss
of esteem in his eyes, if I wasn't
brave. Then, on the beach, the horse
of my terror reared, snorting, frothing,
tossing his head, and would not lower it
until I let my husband go,
and drove to our rented house alone.

The shape of Hokusai's prodigious wave
opening its jaws incarnates
and revives my long-forgotten cowardice
and fear; the boatmen seem to row
with terror's stinging spray
in their dot eyes. Yet, the slopes
of swells and boats, the miniature bent
bald heads of the crews, the frosting on
the silkier billows, the snow of the spume—
which seems to be icing the top
of distant Mt. Fuji—all rhythmically repeat
like epic epithets, like history, perhaps, at last,
returning into legend.

Music for One

Andante, Piano Concerto #21 in C, Mozart

enters
the room

in chords
as deep as eyes.

The piano, coruscating
like fountain jets,
answers from inside
my chest which lifts

and lifts
and falls
and falls and lifts.

My breaths are oars
        sluiced in liquid pearl.

Now, again,
the whole orchestra—

        full wordlessness

overflowing
from one hollow
into another

pouring from river
mouths in glassy
cascades

sheeting down sheer
drops.

Listen

What I need to say
may be faint
as a rustle high
in the feathery bamboo,
though I want to sound
bold as the stalks' off-beat
rhythm sticks in the wind.

I know I fling silence
over my shoulder,
as I turn away,

tired of your glance—

brief as a bird's
before your attention
flies off—

or vague—
as if I were clouds
gliding by.

Let your eyes rest
on my face. Arrest me
in turn. I will burst
from the seed
of myself.

Malaise

What we want when the days
begin to pile up against us—though we mumble
only about work not going well,
about a blister on a heel, and our friends
or lovers sigh "Tell me what you want me
to say"—is instinctive enlightenment
megawatts beyond our own—
a rush of it, revelation opening
like the first-seen broad avenues
of a famous city from the heights.

What we want is not laboriously folded
origami birds made according
to instruction—however clever.
We want wild parrots feathered chartreuse,
scarlet, cyan, bursting from their jungle cover,
carrying astonishing messages
in their beaks.

Avis Poetica

No twitter in the tree directly outside the window through which I gaze—no bluebird, blackbird, warbler, thrush.

I make up an inconclusive crow: clumsy, lumbering, flailing off the ground, too big for its landing gear, landing skittishly, like a small plane, brakes on, ailerons up, up in the air again, down, wheels bouncing.

I key in a rambunctious jay: cocky, squawking, in my face, growling, whistling, chattering, pretending to be a hawk.

I rattle the keys, dreaming up a fractious cubist bird, beak opened on one plane, scrawny toes curled on another, tail feathers fanned into a third. Eye-corner flicker. *Wait.* Something has pushed off from a rebounding twig of the Japanese plum, with a knife toss of glittering wings.

Nothing's the Matter

Babysitting Instructions for the Older Grandparent

Swiftly retie your grandson's sneakers
while he insists "I do it
myself!" Snuggle him into
the car seat, and buckle it
(don't awkward-angle
that doddery knee!),
whisk him from daycare
lickety-split singing "wheels
on the bus wheels on the bus,"
saying "yes!" to every gleeful "TRUCK!"

Praise the tiny Tupperware cups
you must fill with raisins or
Teddy Grahams, and praise the lunchbox
you have to find,
and the bedtime story you have to
read, and the desperate cries
for a third from the crib, "*SNOWY DAY!*
SNOWY DAY!" before the child plummets
to sleep.

Praise falling into the guest bed, exhausted,
with granddad, exhausted, who ran
repeatedly to the slide in the playground
to grab the flame-cheeked, careening boy,
and cleaned and diapered
the fusser's bottom and hustled him
into nighttime footies, and hunted down
that rascal plush pup.

Praise sleepy caressing
and sleepy forgetting gravity
rules; warm flesh will be

ash; granddad's beating heart's
precarious—
when nothing's
the matter
In the Night Kitchen,
or anywhere.

Early Astronomy

My granddaughter tells me with the charm
and certainty of her five years that Jupiter
is "the ice cream planet." "If you stepped on
it, you would sink," she recites, passing on

the disarming metaphor of her "other"
grandma. Her eyes go dreamy when she
envisions Saturn's rings. (My turn: "snow-cone" texture!)
"*Whoa!*" she says when we read that Betelgeuse

could hold a billion of our suns. Undwarfed
by spaces where no human race is,
silences where matter barely whispers,
giggling at the name and unafraid, she's on a ride

like the Flying Unicorn, and just thrilled
with these new proofs the world was made for delight.

Vestigial Mom

They are international, polyglot:
between them speaking
Russian, Latvian, Arabic, French,
German, and a little Farsi and Slovak.
They travel or live abroad
for work, and count among their intimate
friends: Georgians, Kenyans,
Palestinians, Syrians, Kazakhs, Tajiks,
Lebanese, Turks. Yet sometimes I want
to tuck them in, to safety pin them
home like mittens to sleeves, to create
years for them like the Advent
calendars of my childhood Catholic friends,
with good surprises behind each little
door

      because eighty years ago,
not too long before *"Juden, Raus!,"*
my father escaped, leaving behind the cousins
I never met, who look at me
out of the old photos, with my eyes,

      because an Arab host rising
against his oppressor could denounce
my Jewish daughter—"American
Satan!"—or worse,
or Netanyahu bomb his city
while she is there,

      because the "frozen
conflicts" in the lands of the former
U.S.S.R. could thaw and my son
be caught in a flood of ethnic blood.

I want to close the book again
on *The Wild Things* gleaming
their fierce teeth, to pretend
I'm a cloud pursuing *The Runaway Bunny*
turned cloud, to gather my children
into the primal room
of *Goodnight Moon,* brilliant red
and green, warm as a lair
hung with animal fur, against
the arctic out-of-doors.

I want to rush out, as if onto
the street below my window
when I hear the squalls
of a sibling fight,
and bribe the Israelis
and Palestinians, the Chechnyans
and Russians, the Kyrgyz and
Uzbeks, the Sunnis and Shiites,
with whatever I've got—
ice cream and cake, video games, Disneyland—
so they'd just *stop.*

The Laughing Cure

to perpetually circumnavigate the globe,
spreading laughter from continent to continent
—Raffi Khatchadourian, "The Laughing Cure"

A chuckle at the negotiating
table, almost completely
suppressed, like a burp, as Abu Mazen startles
awake, having dreamt
of his oldest son as a child
climbing into his lap
to tweak his ear. And Bibi,
hearing, he thinks, one tiny *hee*
that seems to end in a glottal stop
feels an odd tickle in his throat.
Mahmoud Ahmadinejad, saying
he doesn't know who has told
the crowd there are gays
in Iran, 'cause there are *not,* titters
into his lifted arm. Kim Jong-Il,
stuffed with giant rabbit meat,
giggles as he topples off
his platform shoes.
Myanmar's Than Shwe remembers
a joke told by one of the two Moustache Brothers
he imprisoned, and guffaws. Marxist Mugabe slips
on the marble floor of his 25-bedroom palace
and horse-laughs until he roars.
A great wave, like wind
mowing down wheat across
the American plains, across the vast
breadbasket of Russia, roiling
the Atlantic, making the Pacific seethe, rushes around
the globe. The Janjaweed's Kalashnikovs
shake in their arms as they split

their sides, and tears spill
from their eyes. The Taliban in Kandahar
cackle and shriek and let their AK-47s
fall, as they roll on the floors
of their caves. Al-Qaeda in Peshawar
leave off building their IEDs;
they burst their seams, they pee
in the pants of their salwar kameezes,
they laugh until they drop.

The Braille of Evening

The Older Generation

At first, amidst the blur of tentative
green about to swarm,
these trees seem hung with flags
of creamy bloom. Close up,
it's clear those flags
are ash leaves—hung on through
the winter—trembling in the wind
and hanging on,

some curled tightly inwards—
empty dry cocoons, coquilles,
crustacean shells I think I hear
faintly clicking—

some blanched white
as ghosts, bone white, newly translucent—
their veins the color of ink faded
to brown in scraps
of ancient manuscripts.

In the Golden Vistas Group Home

The tarnished bathroom mirror
is a photographic slide webbed
and starred with mold—
of an unknown face.

On the rickety desk in the hall
envelopes cluster with insoluble
signs, as if tracked over
by a scold of jays.

In an alcove, ledge to ceiling,
there's a mandala
of sun—

its afterglow a lavender moth
suffusing the mind.

In the breezeway stumbled into:
white wind.

Her Vacated House

The mirrors are sheeted.
The chairs and couches
lose their shapes under heavy
covers. Dust congregates
in corners. She is silent
and expressionless
as a dressmaker's model.

But I need little—a door
for entry, a window, however
smeared, for light. I sit
on the draped cushions. Motes swirl
and eddy in wan shafts
of sun warming the rooms
that seem to stir. I pin
remnants, vestiges,
traces to her frame.
A long time, now,
I have been
both ventriloquist
and dummy.

I am accustomed
to the squares of my afternoons,
the *tableau vivant*
at their centers. When they tell me
the house is death's
eminent domain,
I shut my ears.
Windows shine
and windows darken; curtains fill
with light, then flatten. The glow
and shadows on her face
make me dream
she's home.

Raving and Burning

In memory of V. K., 1952-2000

In he comes like a whirlwind ripper
of your still blank pages. He erases the equations
from the blackboard of your life,
steamrolls the wax
of your slate blank, resets all the clocks
to the second of his arrival
where they'll stay. You rage against being plucked
in medias res, clutching anything
to be, maimed, hamstrung, shrunken,
blind, for a month, a week, a day,
an hour, not to be
nothing—and the rose of consciousness falls
like a pressed flower
from a dropped book—
and then you are.

Grief-Shock

You think time should flood,
or swerve, or dry up,
but time—like the metronome clicking
while the poor music student struggles—
does nothing unusual
at all. At this millisecond
when you think this rock dropped
in time's river will break
its arrow, the instant is already sliding
downstream like a froth
of bubbles vanishing in *after*
and *after* and *after,* though you lie at the spot
on the shore—stranded
and despoiled, like a homestead
through which an army has stomped
to the beat of trumpets and drums.

After Her Headstone Is Placed on the
First Anniversary of My Last Aunt's Death

There's an almost architectural darkness
I have inside—a blind-windowed edifice calling me
to feel my way around, mental hands searching
for the walls of wall-lessness,
mental eyes opening
to that darkness.

Near the dusty portal—as if shadowing
the scent of cold into the slow spacious
past—I pass my recent dead,
who seemingly might yet
turn and walk back into
sunshine; I mingle through them,
drinking in their absence,
and move further into the distances
of no distance, until there are places
of a different blackness.

And there I begin to lose
my outlines to the dark,
bristling toward me like the fur
of animals. I grow quiet
as a clock without hands,
and the darkness lightens
to the vaguest hologram
of dampened brightness on the inside
of my eyes.
And then I see
a glistening, faint as a frill
of oar foam across a river
black as sky—

the wet eyes
of my deepest dead, who dwell within
the thickening truth—
before the vista
and the edifice eclipse
like iris wipes
in a film, and I turn back,
flattened, into day.

Resident Dead

I glimpse over the cemetery's stone wall the seasonal window
effect, as I slow, driving on a less-than-everyday route in my
suburban town: paper and real pumpkins all over the grass, a large
scarecrow of raffia and printed cloth by one grave. I have visited
my mother's in the small, largely unadorned Jewish section just
once since she was buried there on a July day long ago. I cannot
imagine bringing plastic bouquets, mylar balloons, butterfly
pinwheels, porcelain lambs and angels like those I remember
decorating most of the flat stones, even a miniature July 4th flag
like the few that waved over the Jewish dead—housewarming
presents for the name-plated doors of death's local habitations.
Yet now my mother's wizened corpse in her coffin floats over the
stones into my mind. The skin is taut on her bones, brown and
papery as the skin of mummies, the mouth drawn back, the few
teeth exposed...

But is skin left? Pleistocene slowness or puffball speed?—I have
no idea of the time to dissolution. Could she still be dressed as I
instructed for the closed coffin service—neither in the customary
white shroud, nor as if she were going out to meet her Maker in
good viewing style: suit, jewelry, pumps—but as if we two were
cheating the Angel and she were going in for a long hospital stay?
The old velour robe, the hospital booties, the floral nightgown—
dust, or mildewed into juice? Dust the chipped pink polish on the
nail of her dangling little finger, which I stroked that last night?
Dust the fleshed finger? Yet "my mother is buried in Olivewood
Cemetery," a *place* to stop, or not. Had she been whisked from
my last glimpse of her on her hospital bed, her ashes scattered
to the atmosphere, to whirl with rocks, and stones, and trees,
would I like my dead nonresident? Or would I have felt a restless
permanent unease, like hers—as she wanders through eternity—
as some rabbis warn? I read somewhere the Romans cut off a
little finger for burial—to ground the spirit?—before they burned
the body.

I clasp that last glimpse, the whole body dressed for a night's
sleep, before it slides under the lid of earth, because it seems
easier for the resurrection I don't believe in to occur with the
rudiments of bones and hair and teeth in the neat package of the
coffin—a kind of Erector set in disassembly, an eternal life kit—
than with dispersed dust lifted and sunk on the winds, spirited
into the heavens and falling again in the rain. As if re-assembly
were an imaginable task for an only semi-great God-I-don't-
believe-in: a jigsaw puzzle after tea in the retirement home rather
than the mystery of the first carbon molecule, Jehovah bending
close to breathe on some random handfuls of dust... A plume
of which I leave behind, the convened atoms of my body
accelerating, bound, right now, where I aim.

Body

Wake me again, indivisible
with liberty, bottles singing
in the milk truck, tipped heels clicking
down my street, and my windows flashed
open to the cloud-quilted sky—
a box-stitched comforter
thrown up to air, squares
translucently edged.

My self is tied
in the chains
of you, silenced
by you,

collapsed down into
an irretrievable black box as you
swerve, droop, fizzle—

oh, don't evict me
after my long lease—

and doctors collect
your measurements, medial,
proximal, pick your locks
with dilators, depressors...

Don't drag me
down like a bale
of shadow!
We're thick as thieves
we two, I'm in the thick
of you—

Give back
my brilliant
ignorance.

The Braille of Evening

The last coins of sunlight flash while I read...half-read...
And I'm still inside, waiting—

preparing for something that takes infinite preparation,
yet may reveal itself at any moment...if I am waiting.

An impish prof once ambled towards me—surrounded by books
      and ash at a dank desk—
and said "It's the cocktail hour! What are you waiting for?"

My ancestors in their black coats and fur hats
were lost in thickets of holy letters, waiting

for Moshiach. Their pages crumbled, their skin
yellowed to parchment while they were waiting.

The quickly brushed luster of the day is drying,
going flat, but still I am waiting.

I imagine leaf-shadow lacework on the grass,
the dog dozing in the sun—no longer waiting

for me—and seeing these so clearly, lift my head,
but cannot read the darkness-gathering trees.

Hallowed Freeze, Exalted Thaw

My years:

a furrow cleaved by a boat
over which the lake heals
over which the ice re-forms,

a contrail streaking across the sky
dissolving like a thought
on the tongue's brink.

I tremble—a drop of water
on the tip of an icicle,
my belly swelling,

I cannot keep my shape.
I will be sublimated to vapor.

Not enough:

pebbles at the empty grave,
at the columbarium,

fleeting reminiscences
in the minds of those still themselves—
speeding and cleaving—

brief condensations
like frost smoke rising
over black holes
in a frozen sea.

Gliding in the Dark

Rothko Dark

like the quiet pool
where I swam, alone,
in a hotel at dusk
in a Northern country,
a somber pool in a barely lit
room, low windows looking out
on the ink sea almost
filling them, a sea
of banked black fire, like the inside
of my eyes, dull sheen
flushed here and there
with the ghost purpling
of an unseen sun—
or my own long looking...

as if—even when immersed
in the soul's darkest
hours—giving one's self
to darkness
faintly lightens it.

La Place de la Cathédrale

How present, how bountiful
and complete the cathedral
in its square onto which
our small hotel's windows
gave, around which we made
our daily promenade, in view of which
we drank our *café crème*. The school girls
on spring vacation sunned and giggled
under the stone harp strings,
and knots of tourists closed and opened
like sea anemones, their cameras flashing
in the dusk like falling stars. And the bells
tolled the bright and the lightless
hours, their quarters, their halves,
their three-quarters...

Too many days, perhaps, but boredom
pleasant, and to consider reduced
choices—the black or blue
sweater, the grey or brown
pants, *petit déjeuner* next door,
or a few doors down, where I studied
the elegant French hound leashed
to a lamppost, head on his paws, meditating
on Nothing, and imagined cultivating
an animal calm.

A sabbath of dedicated
space. Emotions unclotted.
Simpler blood ran
in the arteries, unimpeded by the silt

of years. And the failing
body stopped
failing for an instant,
as if it could keep gliding
in the dark, the bells guiding us
like bell buoys in the voyages
of our sleep.

The Dark

I rose at 2:00 a.m., as I often do,
as our ancestors have been said to—
after their first long nap
starting at nightfall—rising to pray
or talk, back when people spent
more hours under covers, bastioned against
the unlit cold. Half asleep, I walked past
the empty guest room in my dark house, the door
partly closed, wanting, I thought,
a cool glass of water. How miraculous
it was that my bare
feet could find the path
to the kitchen and not stumble
on the dog or the rug or the jutting
bookcase in the hall; how comfortable
this dark was, how dear, a squared-off
compartment of the great dark sweeping
its tide across the globe. And I also thought—
or, felt, really—as I passed,
that something about the angle of the door
seemed purposive, that someone unknown
could be sleeping in that room, which had
briefly housed—after the children left—the various
long-dead: friends or uncles and aunts, or my mother
and father, their chests peacefully rising
and falling.

Maybe I wanted to invite in
someone, some flimsy
flitting ghost for whom
the room would be a kind of ballast.

I poured my water from the pitcher
in the fridge, that cheery welcomer—
like parents putting on the yellow
porch lights for their kids' safe entry
late at night—and drank it while my eyes
began their readjustment to the dark,
then tiptoed past the open door—not quite yet
disappointingly familiar.

Sleep

May you fall into it
groggy and disheveled as a baby
who lets go of his mother's
nipple with a *thwuck*—head lolling,
cowlicks sticking up,
lips open and glistening.

May you fall into it
like a drunk keeling
over onto his own stoop,
having staggered the last possible
step on his slog from the bar.

May you not stand alone
on the shore at 3:00 a.m.,
longing to extricate yourself
from the gritty sand
of consciousness, when everyone
you know has been swept out
by the sea of sleep.

May you reclaim once or twice
the gauze-fine sleep of childhood—
calmly gliding from flickering shadow
to light, from flickering light
to shadow, like a punt
on a tree-lined river.

And may your last be utterly
black and quiet,
and last forever.

After

I take after
my mother, and my mother
is
                    dust

                    from which...
                    to which...

—afterthought
after that
thought: still
me, thinking!—
                    neurons firing,
                    impulses leaping across
                    synaptic clefts, eccentrically networking
                    until

like the language of a last
speaker...mine folds up
like a flag. And there is no one
to receive it. There are no after
words
                    I am translated
                    into stillness.

Afterwards,
I will have stopped
sweating the hours to the top
of the hill, watching them
drain away, pushing them up
again.

Notes

"Immigrant Silences." In German, "*Schweiz*" is Switzerland; "*Wien*" is Vienna. "*Haare: schwartz*" means "hair: black"; "*Augen: dunkel*" means "eyes: dark." "*Zwei Ilgplatz*" means "Two Ilgplatz."

"Neighborly Sorrow." "*Yizkor,*" Hebrew, is a memorial prayer for a departed relative said on that person's "yahrzeit," the anniversary of his or her death (and also a memorial service in the synagogue held several times a year on major holidays). "*Sarahle*" is the Hebrew name Sarah plus the Yiddish affectionate diminutive suffix, "le" (sometimes "ele"); "*Rachele*" is the Hebrew name Rachel plus the diminutive, and "*Rivka*" is the Hebrew name Rebecca.

"Values." "'*Bubbele,*'" Yiddish, is a general term of endearment, i.e. "sweetheart," "honey," "pet."

"Unimaginable." "*Kindertotenlieder,*" *Songs on the Death of Children,* is a song cycle for voice and orchestra composed by Gustav Mahler. The original *Kindertotenlieder* was a collection of over 400 poems written in the 1830s by Friedrich Rückert, following the death of two of his children from scarlet fever; Mahler set five of these to music. *Père Lachaise* is the famous Paris cemetery established in the early nineteenth century and containing the grave sites of many notables with often-elaborate tombs and sculptures.

"Hair." "Monsieur Champagne" was the first celebrity hairdresser in seventeenth-century Paris, for whom the term "coiffeur" was coined.

"What We're Reduced To." "*Luft*" is Yiddish (and German) for "air," with the connotation, here, of "breathable," or "fresh."

"The Braille of Evening." "Moshiach," Hebrew, means "anointed"; the messiah.

Acknowledgments

Grateful acknowledgement is made to the publications in which the following poems originally appeared, sometimes in earlier versions:

2River View: "Brief Reunion"
Adanna: "*La Place de la Cathédrale*"
Avatar Review: "Grief-Shock," "Intimacies," "Sleep"
Cider Press Review: "Hallowed Freeze, Exalted Thaw"
Connotation Press: "At 70," "*Avis Poetica*," "Beyond Request,"
     "Free-Floating Anxiety," "In the Golden Vistas Group Home"
Cyclamens and Swords: "The Heresy of Paraphrase," "*Noblesse*
     Oblige," "*That's* an Unusual Name"
Foundling Review: "Ten Minutes"
How Women Grieve, a special issue of *Adanna*: "After Her
     Headstone Is Placed on the First Anniversary of My Last
     Aunt's Death"
Inlandia: A Literary Journey: "Vestigial Mom"
Innisfree Poetry Journal: "Body," "Early Astronomy," "Music for
     One," "Unimaginable," "What I Love about New York"
JWLA: "Immigrant Silences," "Nothing to Worry About"
Miramar Poetry Journal: "The Dark," "Stirring Banana-Bread
     Batter with My Mother's Spoon"
Mom Egg Review: "Babysitting Instructions for the Older
     Grandparent"
Muse: "Generations"
Pebble Lake Review: "Loved Bodies"
Poemeleon: "Routine Blood Work"
Poetica: "Neighborly Sorrow"
Sequestrum: "After," "Bread," "The Older Generation," "Raving
     and Burning"
Snake Nation Review: "All You Need to Know"
Soundings Review: "The Braille of Evening," "Hair," "Rothko
     Dark"

The New Verse News: "The Laughing Cure," "What We're
    Reduced To"
Theodate: "Hokusai's *Under the Wave off Kanagawa*"
Valparaiso Poetry Review: "Her Vacated House," "Malaise"
West Trestle Review: "Listen"

"At the YW Indoor Spa," first featured online by *Adanna*
(Nov. 15-Jan. 15, 2011-12), appeared in the "Metamorphosis:
Writings About Aging" section of the Good Works anthology
Weatherings (FutureCycle Press, 2015).

"Resident Dead" first appeared in *Bear Flag Republic: Prose Poems
and Poetics from California* (Greenhouse Review/Alcatraz Editions,
2008).

"Values" was first featured online by *Adanna* (Nov. 15-Jan. 15, 2013-
14) and subsequently appeared in *Life and Legends—Fourth Edition:
The Essence of Warriorship* (June 30, 2016).

My sincere thanks to Christopher Buckley and Lavina Blossom,
who read this book in manuscript and provided insightful
suggestions, as well as to the members of my poetry group
(Lavina Blossom, Charlotte Davidson, and Cati Porter) for their
ongoing friendship, conviviality, and helpful commentary on some
of these poems at our meetings. And, as always, my gratitude to
David Kronenfeld, for his faith in, and support of, my endeavors.

*Cover artwork, "The Peasant Wedding" by Pieter Bruegel the Elder
(1566-69, oil on panel); front cover execution by Rey Martinez of the
author's concept; author photo by Michael Elderman; cover and interior
book design by Diane Kistner; Hoefler text and titling*

About FutureCycle Press

FutureCycle Press is dedicated to publishing lasting English-language poetry books, chapbooks, and anthologies in both print-on-demand and Kindle ebook formats. Founded in 2007 by long-time independent editor/publishers and partners Diane Kistner and Robert S. King, the press incorporated as a nonprofit in 2012. A number of our editors are distinguished poets and writers in their own right, and we have been actively involved in the small press movement going back to the early seventies.

The FutureCycle Poetry Book Prize and honorarium is awarded annually for the best full-length volume of poetry we publish in a calendar year. Introduced in 2013, our Good Works projects are anthologies devoted to issues of universal significance, with all proceeds donated to a related worthy cause. Our Selected Poems series highlights contemporary poets with a substantial body of work to their credit; with this series we strive to resurrect work that has had limited distribution and is now out of print.

We are dedicated to giving all of the authors we publish the care their work deserves, making our catalog of titles the most diverse and distinguished it can be, and paying forward any earnings to fund more great books.

We've learned a few things about independent publishing over the years. We've also evolved a unique, resilient publishing model that allows us to focus mainly on vetting and preserving for posterity poetry collections of exceptional quality without becoming overwhelmed with bookkeeping and mailing, fundraising activities, or taxing editorial and production "bubbles." To find out more about what we are doing, come see us at www.futurecycle.org.

The FutureCycle Poetry Book Prize

All full-length volumes of poetry published by FutureCycle Press in a given calendar year are considered for the annual FutureCycle Poetry Book Prize. This allows us to consider each submission on its own merits, outside of the context of a contest. Too, the judges see the finished book, which will have benefitted from the beautiful book design and strong editorial gloss we are famous for.

The book ranked the best in judging is announced as the prize-winner in the subsequent year. There is no fixed monetary award; instead, the winning poet receives an honorarium of 20% of the total net royalties from all poetry books and chapbooks the press sold online in the year the winning book was published. The winner is also accorded the honor of being on the panel of judges for the next year's competition; all judges receive copies of all contending books to keep for their personal library.

www.ingramcontent.com/pod-product-compliance
Lightning Source LLC
Chambersburg PA
CBHW070000100426
42741CB00012B/3094